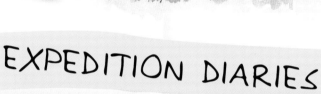

EXPEDITION DIARIES

AFRICAN SAVANNAH

Simon Chapman

W
FRANKLIN WATTS
LONDON · SYDNEY

Expedition to Africa

I'm heading to Botswana in Southern Africa, travelling through the scrubby Kalahari Desert then into the sand dunes of the Namib Desert. (We might also get to the Skeleton Coast.) From there I'll head inland to the dry thorn scrub around the Etosha Pan, where I'm hoping to see both black and southern white rhinos. It won't all be dry and dusty. In the heart of the Kalahari is the Okavango Delta, a vast area of swamps. It is full of wildlife, such as hippos, crocs and elephants, and I'll be exploring just a tiny part of it.

Personal kit list
- Long trousers and long-sleeved shirt - to keep out mosquitoes around the Okavango, and to keep warm during the cold desert nights
- Shorts and T-shirts for the hot days
- Walking boots
- Gilet (waistcoat jacket) with loads of pockets for my diary, paintbrushes, camera, etc
- Sunhat
- Binoculars for watching wildlife

Getting to Botswana
My starting point for entering the Kalahari is a small town called Nata, which is just across the border from Zimbabwe (this is where I'm flying into). For most of my journey I'll be travelling by truck. It'll drive well on the good roads between towns, but it will also manage rough ground too - and there's going to be plenty of that!

KALAHARI BASIN

The Kalahari is a large, basin-like plain stretching 1,600 km (north to south) and 966 km (east to west) across Botswana, Namibia and the Northern Cape in South Africa. The southwestern area of the basin receives less than 250 mm of rain every year. The north-eastern area receives more annual rainfall, but this drains immediately through the deep sand. Conditions in the south-west mean few trees or bushes can survive there, only scattered shrubs and grasses are able to grow. In the northern Kalahari evergreen and deciduous trees dot the landscape. The mix of grassland with scattered trees makes the Kalahari a tropical grassland biome or savannah.

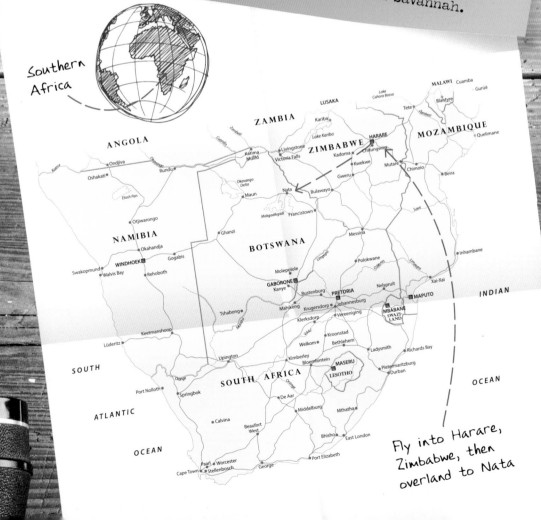

Southern Africa

Fly into Harare, Zimbabwe, then overland to Nata

I've arranged to meet up with James, who runs a 'tour truck' that he's driving to Windhoek for repairs. (Let's hope we don't breakdown before we get there!) We won't be taking the truck off-road much, I'm relying on being able to hike.

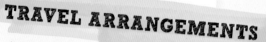

Roof seat

Bed rolls

Sides roll down to keep out dust (or rain, although it shouldn't be wet at this time of year)

Toolkit, water carriers, cooking equipment stored on side of truck

Sand ladders (to put on soft ground if we get bogged down)

Firewood tied to bumper

Fuel tanks

Wildlife can be just as hazardous as the road conditions - especially if it runs out in front of you!

OKAVANGO DELTA

When heavy rains fall in the uplands of central Angola, run-off water creates streams that flow south to form the Okavango River. It flows for 1,600 km to the southeast of the Kalahari, before breaking up into many smaller channels in northern Botswana. These feed the area of swamps known as the Okavango Delta. The delta covers an area of about 16,800 sq km. Papyrus reeds and aquatic plants fill the lower areas of the delta, while patches of woodland and savannah occupy the higher parts.

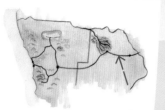

Kalahari Desert

I'm up on the roof seat, as we drive on the road from Nata to Maun. This road skirts the Kalahari Desert, and is like a black line through low scrub and bush, stretching off into the distance.

A couple of times we have driven behind flocks of ostriches running on the road – they run for a while, then veer off. Just now we drove by a cow carcass, scattering huge vultures as we passed.

One bird was a really BIG

mean-looking lappet-faced vulture (*Torgos tracheliotos*).

Apart from the ostriches, most of the journey has been disappointingly wildlife-free, apart from some warthogs, lilac-breasted rollers (sitting on telegraph wires) and southern yellow-billed hornbills perched on termite mounds.

Termite mound. Sometimes you see birds sitting on these.

Southern yellow-billed hornbill (Tockus leucomelas). Black tail with white edge. The underside pattern is strikingly black and white.

Safari camp, Maun, 6.00 PM

We're arriving at the campsite where we'll be staying ...

Ouch! No big trees for miles around, then we get to the campsite and there are loads ... with their branches overhanging the road. I was sitting in the roof seat when I got my arm spiked nastily on an acacia thorn tree. One thorn went in under my left elbow and sliced along ... so now I've got lots of sticky butterfly strips holding the cut together.

LATER ...

This lilac-breasted roller (right) kept gliding down and picking up insects that had been disturbed as we unpacked the tents.

7

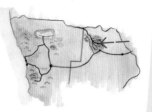

Okavango Delta

20 JUL, just after breakfast

I'm heading out into the bush today where I'll be spending a few days. It's about an hour by motorboat, then another couple of hours by mokoro (a traditional dugout canoe) from a buffalo fence north of Maun. The fence is there to keep the cattle out of the swamps, and keep the wildlife in.

I'm travelling with two Hambukushu guides (Brendan and Socar) who know their way through the wetlands. They use poles to push the canoe along – and **it's very relaxing!** Just now, I missed seeing a hippo as

I was almost falling asleep!

Mid-afternoon, on the Okavango Delta

Skimmers
(*Rynchops flavirostris*)

At one point a large flock of skimmers swooped up as ...

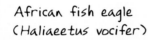

... a fish eagle dived amongst them and grabbed something.

The skimmers fluttered up like black-and-white confetti. Meanwhile, some nearby hippos started thrashing about as the eagle snatched up its prey and flapped to a riverside tree.

African fish eagle
(*Haliaeetus vocifer*)

Late afternoon

I have seen five elephants and lots of lechwe antelope (*Kobus leche*).

Punting towards our camping place (I hope) and it's really atmospheric with yellow, late afternoon light on the reeds, jungle noises and a full Moon in the sky.

LATER...

After dark, sitting in our camp.
The night noises from the reed beds nearby are very loud — there's a huge frog chorus going on!

FIRE!

My sleep was interrupted by the crackling sound of a **very large FIRE!** close to the tent.

Brendan was trying to scare off two elephants that had come too close to the camp. I didn't see the elephants, I just saw the savannah ablaze.

Whole bushes were erupting into FLAME.

Right now, Socar is beating down flames while shouting at Brendan for being so reckless. I'm going to help ... Luckily, we stamp out the fire.

21 JUL, morning

Just found a mouse in my rucksack!

It was tiny with big dark eyes, and it looked so cute. It had nibbled through a plastic bag containing some bread rolls. I headed out on a walk from our camp. There are lots of reedbuck, impala and some warthogs around.

The best bit for me was coming across a red lechwe buck (left) drinking at a swampy lake, with two wattled cranes nearby. The antelope was unaware of us and we managed to creep up close. Red lechwe bucks run with their heads down, as if their horns are too heavy.

They bound along in a series of jumps.

Tsessebe (Damaliscus lunatus)

7.00 PM, back at camp

We're sitting around the fire baking potatoes and listening to frogs.

Socar hurt his ankle in the morning, so our afternoon trek was at a slower pace. Much of the land around had been burned deliberately (to promote the growth of new grass shoots, according to Brendan).

Even so, we saw a mixed herd of 40–50 wildebeest, zebra and tsessebe, and also saw reedbuck (above), lechwe and one giraffe. When the herd started moving, the antelope sent up clouds of dust. You could really imagine a wildebeest migration.

Bush Walk

22 JUL, sunrise

Last night we were kept awake by lions roaring near our campsite. James (the truck driver) said that if our guides come across lions (or a leopard) we should do what they do.

If they run away, then we should run faster!

4 PM, on bush walk with Brendan

My heart is pounding! We've been following a leopard that we could hear up ahead.

It kept making a coughing call. We tracked it through thick bushes and under low trees, but made too much noise and lost it. Now I think about it, pursuing a leopard doesn't sound like a clever idea – but it would have been great to have seen it.

Female Impala
(Aepyceros melampus)

Afterwards, we could see a baboon howling from a tree to our left, some tsessebe, a wildebeest and a herd of impala.

We got to about 100 m from the impala before they headed off.

HIPPOPOTAMUS
(HIPPOPOTAMUS AMPHIBIOUS)

Hippos are large, semi-aquatic mammals that live in eastern, central and parts of southern Africa. They enjoy basking along the banks of rivers and lakes during the heat of the day, and feeding on surrounding grasses at dusk. Adults can weigh up to 1,500 kg.

23 AUG, morning

Travelling back to the campsite in the canoe, we give hippos lots of space.

They have been known to sink boats, and are more dangerous than the crocodiles. Crocs would only go for you if you're already in the water.

This big, mean-looking croc was resting on the bank.

There are lots of blacksmith plovers (*Vanellus armatus*, right) on the shoreline. The bird got its name from the 'plink-plinking' noise it makes when calling. It sounds like a blacksmith striking a hammer on metal.

Bird's Eye View

When I got back from the Okavango Delta, I hopped on a light aircraft and flew across the wetlands.

It was late afternoon and the yellow light really lit up the trees and marshes.

We swooped low over reed beds,

scattering lechwe, and flew past hundreds of buffalo. There were lots of elephants and hippos wallowing in the water. One had its mouth gaping open in true hippo style!

From the air I could see the fringes of wilderness marked abruptly by the straight line of the buffalo fence, separating the wildlife from farmers' cattle. These fences used to prevent the seasonal mass migration of wildlife, leading to the deaths of millions of animals (through thirst and when they became entangled in the wire), but many fences have now been taken down.

MIGRATION

Wildlife in Botswana, including zebras, wildebeest, buffalo and elephants move across the land according to the seasons: spending the driest months near to the rivers and then moving to the grasslands of the Kalahari for the wetter months. They move in large numbers across huge distances at different times of the year.

25 AUG, driving towards the Tsodilo Hills

I'm driving west with James, on our way to Windhoek. We're surrounded by endless views of low, scrubby bush. While taking a break I spotted a jackal chasing a vulture away from a carcass. There were also a couple of tawny eagles (*Aquila rapax*) at first, too. Then two lappet-faced vultures

SWOOPED

in and started fighting.

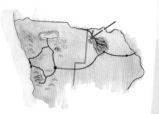

Tsodilo Hills

Very quick sketch of long-horned cattle at a cattle station where we are refilling the jerry cans with water.

Hordes of cows are clustered around a hand pump, sending up clouds of dust. I was quite scared I would be impaled on the horns of one that suddenly swung around as I sketched.

SOIL EROSION

Soil erosion can occur due to drought, deforestation, fires and the overgrazing of farm animals in one area. Cattle graze and trample on plants and these plants are not allowed time to grow and recover. As a result, the plants die and the soil below them is washed or blown away by rain and wind, causing what's known as desertification; where once fertile land becomes desert-like.

We stopped off at a 'bushman village' - consisting of traditional rondavel huts.

It's a tourist destination, and I felt really awkward – with so many wealthy tourists pestering the villagers. The bushmen led a nomadic life, travelling through the bush – and some still do – though not here.

Late afternoon

Today, we've driven on rough sandy roads towards a group of hills that stick out of a huge flat expanse of bush.

The horizon is flat and sandy grey on all sides. A crazy francolin (right) kept running ahead of the truck. It stayed in front without ducking to the side for over 100 metres!

17

Exploring Caves

26 JUL, afternoon, rocky outcrop
in the Tsodilo Hills

Lucky escape!

I've just done five hours trekking around with a full pack and four litres of water (now all drunk ... and I'm still thirsty).

I had a close encounter with a metre-wide rock. It toppled as I was clambering over it, and I gashed my knee when I dived to the side to avoid the boulder as it fell. The wound is taking ages to dry off, and I'm being dive-bombed by bees. (As I'm writing this two curious francolins are staring at me!)

Back at camp

A group of warthogs skirted round the camp, and I managed to sketch them while they were grazing.

This big, mean-looking male warthog got a bit close, which explains why his ear looks a bit

wobbly – because I was
SHAKING!

Warthogs run with their tails in the air like aerials, and kneel down on the ground to feed.

Our camp backs on to a cliff face of jumbled rocks and caves. I climbed up between the rocks with James. At some points it was quite a squeeze! I picked up a couple of long black-and-white striped porcupine quills (actually one stuck into me). Perhaps the porcupine has been sleeping here?

TSODILO HILLS
In north-west Botswana, near the Namibian border, lies a 10 km area of rock containing over 4,500 rock art paintings. Tsodilo Hills is a UNESCO World Heritage site. The paintings give an insight into life in the area over the last 100,000 years. Local people consider it to be an important place of worship and spiritual area.

LATER...

There's a hyena at the edge of camp, lured by the bones from a goat we had for dinner. I really got a shock when I realised it was just behind me.

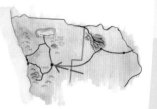

Namib Desert

27 JUL, long drive to Windhoek, capital of Namibia

Heading towards the Namib Desert – Etosha is still about a week away. Apart from being spiked by the quill yesterday,

I thought I had made it through the rocky passages unscathed. I've discovered today, after hours of bumping along dirt roads, that my back was badly grazed and bruised.

I saw this martial eagle (Polemaetus bellicosus) early in the morning.

28 JUL

I'm leaving James today, and hitching a ride with Paul.

We're now heading south from Windhoek in his sand-blasted truck. When we stop for a rest break there are kudu with huge spiral horns in the scrub, sheltering from the Sun amongst some stunted trees.

Namibia is such an unpopulated country. Outside Windhoek, we have passed hardly any houses. Paul pointed out that there are two types of fence alongside the roads:

- For cattle, regular fence posts with barbed wire along the top
- For game, three or four strands of wire with some of the poles connected to the top wires only. Game includes antelope, such as kudu, which is hunted for meat. You can buy dried meat called 'Biltong'. (It keeps for ages and makes great trail rations.)

It's really windy; like a sandstorm outside. I hope the tent doesn't blow away! It has been a long, tiring drive. The changing scenery is getting more desert-like as we travel south-west.

Earlier, we travelled across a flat semi-desert plain. This opened out after we followed a twisting valley that was noticeably greener than anywhere else I have seen in Namibia so far. There was even running water in some parts of the stream bed.

LATER...

Found a scorpion under my tent. I looked it up in a book about southern African wildlife. It's a deadly one.

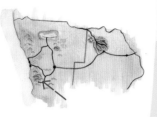

Desert Life

Sossusvlei, dawn, up a sand dune

We climbed up here to catch the sunrise, and it was hard work, as you slip down slightly with each step you take.

It's FREEZING!

I'm being sandblasted, but the view is spectacular. Some of the dunes here are the tallest in the world, reaching 300–400 m!

NAMIB DESERT

The Namib is a coastal desert on the west coast of southern Africa. It is 81,000 sq km in size and borders the Atlantic Ocean. The desert is made up of gravel plains, mountains and huge sand dunes. Some wildlife, such as the fog-basking darkling beetle or the welwitschia plant, can access moisture along the coast from early morning sea fog.

Massive sand dunes, like huge orange waves.

29 JUL, 9.30 AM, Deadvlei

I'm at a white clay pan that was once a shallow lake.

The water has been cut off by the shifting dunes, killing any trees, so now the only plants that grow here are clumps of salsola and nara. These survive on moisture from morning mist.

So much salty sand blowing in the wind – stinging my eyes. (I am writing this with my T-shirt over my face.) I saw a couple of **black-backed jackals (Canis mesomelas) trying to find shelter.**

The only other life here seems to be

darkling beetles wandering over the dunes.

They climb to the top of the dunes when fog blows in from the coast, and get drenched with moisture. Not today though – it's cloudless ...

30 JUL, short stop near Solitaire

At a junction with unrusted (as it's too dry) wrecked vintage cars by the roadside.

The terrain is totally parched – just vast flats of gravel with scattered weeds. It's grey and dry.

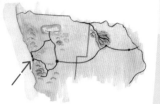

Skeleton Coast

Out on the coast it's hard to believe that just an hour ago we were in

baking hot desert.

Behind the mudflats, with lesser and greater flamingos, are expensive villas with sprinklers on their green lawns. There are smartly dressed people walking dogs on the coastal strip – and a surprising amount of dead, dismembered flamingos lying around (which could be down to the jackals). It's not the dead birds that give this coast its name though, but rather the number of wrecked ships that wash up here.

SKELETON COAST NATIONAL PARK

This National Park stretches along the Namibian coast for 500 km, from the Kunene River to the Ugab River. Rough seas, sea fog and a strong sea current have caused many shipwrecks along the shore, and whales become stranded here, too. As a result, the area is littered with whale bones and long-abandoned ships.

24

WALVIS BAY

Walvis Bay is a coastal city of 100,000 people in Namibia. Its sheltered, deep harbour makes it a busy stopping-off point for fishing boats and ships. Birdlife, including flamingos and pelicans, fill the Walvis Bay Lagoon. Dune 7 lies on the outskirts of the town. Rising up 383 m from its base, Dune 7 is one of the highest sand dunes in the world.

Swakopmund (next coastal town along), late afternoon

The campsite where I'm stopping off is in a housing estate. Each pitch has its own shower and toilet block. This feels so weird!

Swakopmund Town* was an important harbour when Namibia was 'German South-West Africa' a century ago. Now, this little beach resort does not feel like part of Namibia. Then again, it doesn't feel very German either.

* This town was made famous when film star Angelina Jolie gave birth to her daughter Shiloh there.

25

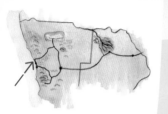

Seal Reserve

1 AUG, morning, driving up the Skeleton Coast

Nearby someone has written 'skeleton coast' in sea shells, and made a skeleton on the sand using seal ribs and a dolphin skull.

Wreck of the Zelia - a fishing trawler that ran aground.

The coastal desert here really is very wind- and salt-blasted.

There is just flat gravel all around, but if you look closely there are small stones with colourful lichens growing on them.

A sign by the road says you must not tread on the lichen because it is so fragile, and takes years to grow back.

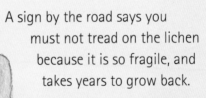

CAPE CROSS SEAL RESERVE

Cape Cross Seal Reserve is found close to Swakopmund, where more seals breed than anywhere else in the world. During the breeding season (November to December) up to 210,000 seals can be found at Cape Cross. The cold, nutrient-rich Benguela Current provides many fish for the seals, orca and sharks, while kelp gulls, cormorants and the Damara tern soar above the waves.

This part of the rocky coast is a haven for seals and sea lions. Southern fur seals congregate at the Cape Cross sea lion colony. Beyond the crashing waves and surf, hundreds of sea lions play in the water, some on their sides with their flippers in the air. There are females and young here on the shore ... oh,

what a stink!

2 PM, driving inland

Suddenly, an ostrich seemed to almost appear out of nowhere by the roadside.

Also found this male welwitschia plant. These are incredible plants – really very unique – and slow growing. The male plants are a salmon colour, while the female ones are green, and can live for up to a whopping 2,000 years!

27

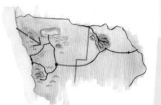

Erongo and Kunene

I'm staying on a cheetah farm in a region that was called Damaraland* during apartheid. I've just been

licked by a Cheetah!

This was one of four tame cheetahs at the farm. Maybe because I hadn't had a shower recently and had salty sweat on me, the cheetah came over and started

licking my legs.

At first I thought it was nibbling me. Its tongue was like really rough sandpaper – quite unpleasant – but I didn't want to make any sudden moves or upset it.

Cheetahs are surprisingly big and mean-looking when you have one sandpapering your knees and nuzzling your thigh.

* Now called the Erongo region and the Kunene region.

I'm standing in the back of a pickup truck watching semi-wild cheetahs being fed in a huge enclosure. The bush country is quite thick and thorny here. That means when the big cats charge down their prey, they often get spiked in the face by the bushes. Local farmers injure the cheetahs, too. At the cheetah farm the cats are cared for, before being released.

This was the first of two cheetahs that we saw.

The Cheetah Conservation Fund is giving big Anatolian dogs to goat farmers to help protect their flocks from cheetah attacks; the dogs bark, scaring the cats away and the farmers don't shoot the cats.

Road to Etosha, early afternoon

The wild north-west of Namibia really feels like the middle of nowhere.

The total desolation of the coastal desert has given way to scrubby hills. There are more bushes and straggly trees along dry water courses, but it's certainly not lush and green. Sylvia, the guide back at the cheetah conservation farm, said it hasn't rained in two years.

Occasionally, we see people from the truck, like these Herero children (above). We have seen one hut in the distance, but no villages.

29

Road to Etosha

The colouring of the giraffes varies a lot. Some are very pale, while others are very dark brown or reddish.

The blotches aren't random. You can follow the lines of lighter colour between them.

Twyfelfontein, Khoisan rock art

The rock art in this valley has been created over thousands of years, with examples dating back 10,000 years. There are images of giraffes, ostriches and rhinoceroses, and coastal animals too, including seal lions. Many are painted in red ochre, while others are etched into the sandstone.

This one is called 'Lion Man' as it has five toes. The ancient hunters or shamen who painted this would have known that lions have four toes, so is this meant to be half lion, half man? Who knows!

30

Paul is heading to a Himba village this morning, although I have mixed feelings about this.

The village is one of a number visited by tourists, and while the people receive money they bring in, I wonder how much they actually benefit.

Some women have their skin coated with red ochre (symbolising earth and blood), and have red clay smeared on their hair in the traditional way.

Their jewellery is made from materials including **leather, grass, cloth, copper and ostrich shell.**

The guide told us that the Himba have managed to preserve their identity, and campaigned against development of a hydroelectric dam along the Kunene River, which would have flooded their lands.

31

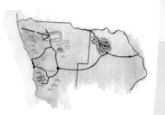

3 AUG, afternoon

I've just seen two black rhinos!

This is before I get into the national park. I thought there were warthogs behind the bushes, but they were too big.

They briefly ran parallel to the truck before pushing away from us through a gap in the thorn-scrub.

BLACK RHINO
(DICEROS BICORNIS)

Both the white rhino and the smaller black rhino are found in Africa. Hunted and killed for their horns, black rhinos are critically endangered, with a world population of around 5,000. They are found in savannah grasslands, woodlands and wetlands. Black rhinos are herbivores, reaching 1.5 m in height and weighing up to 1,400 kg.

I'm staying in the park for the next couple of days. Right now, I'm looking out over desolate tufty grassland, with a white salt pan behind. When it rains, this becomes a vast salty lake. There are lots of zebra here, wildebeest and a couple of impala.

Each Burchell's zebra (Equus quagga burchellii) has a unique stripe pattern.

4 AUG, 8.30 AM

I've been dropped at a game-viewing platform overlooking a waterhole to catch early risers.

I can hardly write as it's so cold. There's just one jackal here at the moment, though earlier I did see a giraffe and hyena amble past.

LATER...

This large bull elephant came down to drink. There was also another younger bull, full of bravado, quick to flap his ears and look angry.

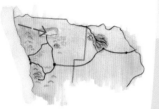

At The Water Hole

Two-and-a-half hours later
and it's still windy and cold,
but I've seen so much wildlife.

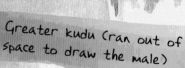

Greater kudu (ran out of
space to draw the male)

Right now there are

over 25 blue wildebeest grazing.

It is just spectacular.
They are really close,
with their manes and tails
flapping in the wind.

I've been out on a game count with a zoologist who's from Maryland University in the USA. I spent a couple of hours this morning, and about an hour yesterday, noting down species and

direction of movement of the herds of antelope and zebra around the waterhole.

ETOSHA PAN

The Etosha Pan is a flat salt pan in northern Namibia. The Kunene River used to flow south, forming a huge lake. Since then, the river changed its course, leaving a dry pan of salt, sand and mud. Few plants grow here, other than a blue-green algae and some grasses.

The water hole is man-made and filled by a pump that draws water up from a borehole. The problem is that grazers, like the zebra, overgraze the land in the pan and trample it to dust.

The zoologist's research is to find out if the waterholes can be left dry for a season to allow the vegetation around them to regrow. At night, another group continued the count using night vision equipment. I was really hoping to get on a night count, but the men there this morning looked totally frozen, so I'm glad I didn't.

Red-winged pratincole (Glareola pratincola) swooping low as it hunts for flying insects.

35

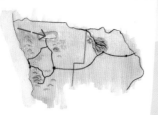

Park Drive

This morning I'm out in the park with Jabalo, one of the drivers here. We're watching a mother black rhino and her baby drinking at the water's edge.

Earlier, the baby was suckling from her. Right now, the rhinos are hanging back and a bull elephant has come into drink. A third rhino has just arrived. The male had a brief stand-off with the female.

She bellowed, then turned her back.

We have seen so many black rhinos now. Jabalo commented,

"That's a lot of money
walking around over there."

Seeing so many rhinos makes you forget how rare they have become because of ivory poachers.

36

I'm desperate to go walking through the bush, especially the woodland savannah. It's much more exciting than being in a vehicle, but the risk from lion attack is just too high here.

I'm watching two lions right now, dozing under a bush with a group of springbok close by, and some giraffes browsing low acacia scrub.

Night drive

Jabalo has taken me out for a night drive to spot lions.

I didn't expect we'd have much luck as it's so cold. I have all my clothes on and a blanket wrapped around me, and

I'm freezing!

But we got more than I bargained for. Three lions padded right up to our Land Rover! I was in so much shock that by the time I had got out my sketch pad, they had sat down.

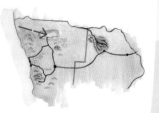

Wildlife spotting

6 AUG

I'll be leaving Etosha tomorrow to start heading back via Waterberg, but before I go ...

I saw this red hartebeest.
They are only found in southern Africa.

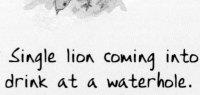

Single lion coming into drink at a waterhole.
After drinking, this lion made a point of spray marking (weeing) then kicking back on the place where he had just reached the water so other lions know:

"This is my drinking place. Keep away!"

Drinking giraffe

apparently done in short bursts because:

- They are vulnerable to predators when their heads are down.

- They have to shut off the blood vessels to stop all the blood in the neck flowing down into their heads. It raises its head again when it starts to hurt.

At sunset, spotted this black-backed jackal (Canis mesomelas) trotting in with head held low to bother Egyptian geese (*Alopochen aegyptiaca*).

Mountain Hike

Mid-morning, on road to Windhoek

I've got a lift this morning with an American couple, and we've stopped at a rocky plateau on the way back towards Windhoek.

Clouds! There are clouds in the sky

for (almost) the first time since I've been in Namibia.

Hiking up to the plateau (above) we climbed into high forest through a cleft in the cliff edge, which is populated by colonies of rock hyrax.

ROCK HYRAX
(PROCAVIA CAPENSIS)

Rock hyrax are small, tailless mammals that can grow up to 55 cm long, and weigh 4.7 kg. They have brown-grey fur, with a lighter-coloured belly and a pair of small pointed tusks in the upper part of their mouth. They feed on grasses and leaves and are found across Africa and the Middle East.

I sat by a stream with a trickle of water running down (just about the first running water I've seen in Namibia, which I suppose is why they call this place 'Waterberg' – water mountain). No matter how hard I try, I can't avoid making my hyrax sketch look like a cartoon character! Three just popped their heads up and spent a long time looking at me.

We carried on up to the top, and saw more rock art featuring elongated figures (like the one on the left from the Tsodilo Hills). It might not sound much, but the highlight for me was finding rhino, giraffe and buffalo spoor (polite word for poo) on the hike.

LATER...

We heard what might have been a leopard, which prompted us to head back to the car ...

41

Waterberg Plateau

7 AUG, 8.30 AM, walking up a valley

I've camped in Waterberg Park, and am following

a trail that I hope leads along the sloping valley side, right up to the plateau's top edge.

I'll then loop around until I get to a stream bed, and follow that back down to the valley. There are dozens of birds around, especially red-billed hornbills (*Tockus erythrorhynchus*, below), and I just now flushed out a really russet-coloured bushbuck (*Tragelaphus scriptus sylvaticus*).

Eroded sandstone rock in the park creates spectacular formations.

Afternoon

I got genuinely unnerved before drawing this little sketch. That's why it's a bit 'shaky'.

I was walking down a dry stream bed towards the campsite, when I heard a rustling in the bushes to my left. It seemed to be following me. I could hear a deep barking up ahead, and that turned out to be baboons.

WATERBERG PLATEAU

This table mountain rises 420 m up out of the Kalahari, in eastern Namibia. The red sandstone cliffs are surrounded by savannah. Over 200 species of bird, including the rare Cape vulture, and 25 species of mammal, including black and white rhino, buffalo and giraffe, make this area their home. The area has been a nature reserve since 1972.

But, when I turned around there were three or four buffalo, probably more. As I slowly got my sketch pad out, a big male stood facing me and snorted.

My hands were shaking so much I nearly dropped my pencil!

6.00 PM, at a waterhole

There are sandgrouse arriving for water, and at least 28 buffalo.

One fairly large youngster keeps trying to suckle, but its mother gets annoyed and sits down. Some of the buffalo are fairly 'snorty' and annoyed with each other.

43

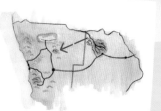

White Rhinos

8 AUG, Waterberg Park, sunset

I am freezing cold again after being out looking for rhinos.

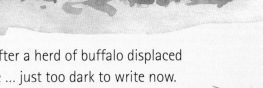

I saw some elands (*Taurotragus oryx*) earlier with their lumpish, rather than graceful movement.
They were at the edge of a waterhole, after a herd of buffalo displaced them. There were also four giraffes here ... just too dark to write now.

Last day in Waterberg

I'm with a guide, Daniel JJ, tracking white rhino.

The southern white rhino we saw was **huge** – about the size of a van – and much bigger than the black rhinos I saw at Etosha.

Daniel JJ and me tracking rhino.

We tracked it by looking for its fist-sized poo. Moist droppings meant it had to be quite near.

We had to loop around so we were upwind of the rhino, and our scent would blow away from us. That meant we could smell it –

whoo! A bit whiffy!

Finally, it shuffled through the thorn bushes until it was about 10 m away. That was close enough, thank you! Then its nerve gave, and it reversed backwards before crashing away. **Amazing!**

Didn't see the rhino again, but the walk back was an adventure in itself, with zebras, kudus and even a couple of giraffes around us.

LATER...

Important things to do now. I have two days until my flight home from Windhoek – and that's still 300 km away. Need to sort some transport – ASAP!

Amazingly, I made my flight home. When I got back to the campsite a few tourist cars had turned up, so I just asked around.

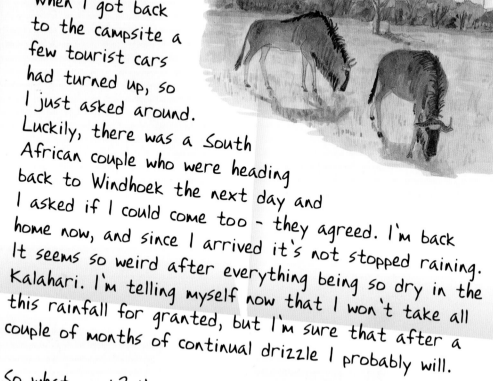

Luckily, there was a South African couple who were heading back to Windhoek the next day and I asked if I could come too – they agreed. I'm back home now, and since I arrived it's not stopped raining. It seems so weird after everything being so dry in the Kalahari. I'm telling myself now that I won't take all this rainfall for granted, but I'm sure that after a couple of months of continual drizzle I probably will.

So what next? I've been to 'dry Africa', so I'll try it in the wet season!

Postscript. It was a good plan. My next trip to Africa was to explore the steaming savannahs and rainforests of Gabon in the centre of the continent. I tracked gorillas, crept right up to bright orange 'red river hogs' (which are like jungle warthogs) and found that you can get frighteningly close to an elephant if it decides to stand still behind a tree.

ETOSHA NATIONAL PARK

The Etosha Pan is at the centre of the Etosha National Park in Namibia. At 22,269 km in size (half the size of Switzerland), the park is a huge wildlife sanctuary for lions, elephants, rhinoceros, elands, zebras and springbok. There is abundant bird life, including flamingos, vultures, hawks, eagles and ostriches.

Tree-savannah vegetation dominates the east of the park, including wild fig and date palms. Thorn-shrub savannah in the west of the park includes moringa trees. The park is an important tourist centre in Namibia, being one of the best places to view almost all of Africa's famous wildlife.

Glossary

biome Regions of the world with a similar climate, plants and animals, such as deserts, forests, oceans, grasslands.

carcass The dead body of an animal.

colony a community of animals or plants of one kind living closely together.

deciduous A tree or shrub that sheds its leaves every year.

deforestation The clearance of forests or trees from an area.

delta The area at the mouth of a river before it enters the sea.

endangered At risk of extinction.

evergreen A tree or shrub that keeps its leaves throughout the year.

fertile Able to produce plenty of growth.

grassland A biome where there is enough water for grasses to grow, but not enough for trees to survive.

herbivore An animal that feeds on plants.

hydroelectric Relating to the generation of electricity using the flow of water.

impaled To pierce with something sharp.

lichen A simple plant that grows as a crust on rocks, walls and trees.

migration The movement of animals from one place to another.

nomadic Description of people who travel from place to place, who have no permanent home.

nutrient A substance living things need to grow.

plateau An area of high, level ground.

savannah A type of grassland biome, with scattered trees and a variety of grasses.

semi-aquatic Living in or near water for some of the time.

swamp An area of low-lying ground where water collects.

UNESCO (United Nations Educational Scientific and Cultural Organization) an agency set up by the UN to promote the exchange of ideas and culture.

Index

Franklin Watts
First published in Great Britain in 2018 by
The Watts Publishing Group

Copyright © The Watts Publishing Group 2018

All rights reserved

Executive editor: Adrian Cole
Series designer: Elaine Wilkinson
Design manager: Peter Scoulding
Picture researcher: Diana Morris

Photo acknowledgements:
All illustrations and photos S. Chapman except: AndreAnita/Shutterstock: 45cr. Stephen Butler/Shuttertock: 42br. Henk Bogaard/Shutterstock: 23bl. cpaulfell/Shutterstock: 17br. EcoPrint/Shutterstock: 13b. CarGe/Shutterstock: 31bl. Michal Cerny/Alamy: marzia franceschini/Shutterstock: 24br. Paula French/Shutterstock: 39bl. Anna Efimova/Shutterstock: 32bl. 2–3bg, 4–5bg, 46–47bg, 48bg. Chris Jenner/Shutterstock: 37tl. Halfpoint/Shutterstock: 1bg, Franco Locato/Shutterstock: 12tr. francesco de marco/Shutterstock: 25br. Rainer Lesniewski/Shutterstock: 3b. 28cl. Jacqui Martin/Shutterstock: 6bl, 7t, 8cl, 8tr, 8br, 10tr, 11cr, 12bl, 13cr, 14br, 15tr, 16tr, 16br, 18tr, 18br, 19tr, 20br, 21br, 22tr, 24cl, 25tr, 25cr, 27tr, 27bl, 27br, 28bl, 29tr, 30cl, 31cr, 32br, 33cr, 34br, 35tr, 35br,36cl, 36br, 37tr, 38tr, 38bl, 39br,40br, 41tr,42bl, 43cr, 44tr, 44br, 45br. Guilherme Mesquita/Shutterstock: 37br. meunierd/Shutterstock: 29br. mezzotint/Shutterstock: 22bl. David Steele/Shutterstock: 3t. Villiers Steyn/Shutterstock: 15trb. Ignatius Tan/Shutterstock: 34bl.
Every attempt has been made to clear copyright. Should there be any inadvertent omission please apply to the publisher for rectification.

ISBN 978 1 4451 5686 6

Printed in China

Franklin Watts
An imprint of Hachette Children's Group
Part of The Watts Publishing Group
Carmelite House
50 Victoria Embankment
London EC4Y 0DZ

An Hachette UK Company
www.hachette.co.uk

www.franklinwatts.co.uk

MIX
Paper from responsible sources
FSC® C104740
FSC
www.fsc.org